AF219588

Impressum
Verlag: BABADADA GmbH, Nedderfeld 112 , 22529 Hamburg
Geschäftsführer / Verlagsleitung: Harald Hof
Druck: Books on Demand GmbH, In de Tarpen 42, 22848 Norderstedt

Imprint
Publisher: BABADADA GmbH, Nedderfeld 112 , 22529 Hamburg, Germany
Managing Director / Publishing direction: Harald Hof
Print: Books on Demand GmbH, In de Tarpen 42, 22848 Norderstedt

除 divide

186/2

教室 classroom

黑板 board

校园 school yard

老师 teacher

纸 paper

书写 write

钢笔 pen

办公桌 desk

直尺 ruler

书 book

学生 pupil

书包
satchel

铅笔盒
pencil case

铅笔
pencil

卷笔刀
pencil sharpener

橡皮擦
rubber

画板
drawing pad

图画

drawing

画笔

paintbrush

颜料盒

paint box

剪刀

scissors

胶水

glue

练习册

exercise book

家庭作业

homework

12

数字

number

2+2

加

add

5-2

减

subtract

2×2

乘

multiply

计算

calculate

A

字母

letter

ABCDEFG
HIJKLMN
OPQRSTU
VWXYZ

字母表

alphabet

字

word

课文

text

读

read

粉笔

chalk

上课

lesson

登记

register

考试

exam

证书

certificate

校服

school uniform

教育

education

百科全书

encyclopedia

大学

university

显微镜

microscope

地图

map

废纸筐

waste-paper basket

酒店
hotel

青年旅社
hostel

外币兑换处
bureau de change

手提箱
suitcase

汽车
car

语言

language

是/否

yes / no

好的

Okay

您好

hello

翻译员

translator

谢谢

Thank you

……多少钱？

how much is…?

我不明白

I do not understand

问题

problem

晚上好！

Good evening!

早上好！

Good morning!

晚安！

Good night!

再见

bye bye

方向

direction

行李

luggage

包

bag

双肩包

backpack

客人

guest

房间

room

睡袋

sleeping bag

帐篷

tent

旅游信息

tourist information

海滩

beach

信用卡

credit card

早餐

breakfast

午餐

lunch

晚餐

dinner

票

ticket

电梯

lift

邮票

stamp

边界

border

海关

customs

大使馆

embassy

签证

visa

护照

passport

交通运输
transport

飞机
aeroplane

船
ship

消防车
fire engine

卡车
truck

公交车
bus

汽艇
motorboat

自行车
bike

汽车
car

摆渡船
ferry

小船
boat

摩托车
motorbike

警车
police car

赛车
racing car

租车
rental car

拼车

car sharing

拖车

breakdown truck

垃圾车

refuse truck

发动机

motor

汽油

fuel

加油站

petrol station

交通标志

traffic sign

交通

traffic

交通堵塞

traffic jam

停车场

car park

火车站

train station

轨道

tracks

火车

train

电车

tram

货车

carriage

直升机

helicopter

机场

airport

塔

tower

乘客

passenger

集装箱

container

纸板箱

carton

手推车

cart

篮子

basket

起飞/降落

take off / land

城市

city

村庄

village

市中心

city centre

房子

house

电影院
cinema

广告
advert

路灯
street lamp

CINEMA

街道
street

出租车
taxi

行人
pedestrian

小吃店
snack shop

人行道
pavement

斑马线
zebra crossing

垃圾箱
bin

十字路口
crossing

红绿灯
traffic lights

小屋

hut

公寓

flat

火车站

train station

市政厅

town hall

博物馆

museum

学校

school

大学
university

银行
bank

医院
hospital

酒店
hotel

药房
pharmacy

办公室
office

书店
book shop

商店
shop

花店
florist's

超市
supermarket

市场
market

百货商店
department store

鱼店
fishmonger's

购物中心
shopping centre

海港
harbour

公园

park

长凳

bench

桥

bridge

楼梯

stairs

地铁

underground

隧道

tunnel

公交车站

bus stop

酒吧

bar

餐馆

restaurant

邮筒

postbox

路标

street sign

停车计时器

parking meter

动物园

zoo

游泳馆

swimming pool

清真寺

mosque

农场
farm

污染
pollution

墓地
graveyard

教堂
church

操场
playground

寺庙
temple

地形
landscape

树叶
leaf

指示牌
signpost

路
way

草地
meadow

石头
stone

树
tree

徒步旅行者
hiker

河
river

草
grass

花
flower

峡谷

valley

山

hill

湖

lake

森林

forest

沙漠

desert

火山

volcano

城堡

castle

彩虹

rainbow

蘑菇

mushroom

棕榈树

palm tree

蚊子

mosquito

苍蝇

fly

蚂蚁

ant

蜜蜂

bee

蜘蛛

spider

地形 - landscape

甲虫

beetle

青蛙

frog

松鼠

squirrel

刺猬

hedgehog

野兔

hare

猫头鹰

owl

鸟

bird

天鹅

swan

野猪

boar

鹿

deer

麋鹿

moose

水坝

dam

风力发电机

wind turbine

太阳能电池板

solar panel

气候

climate

服务员
waiter

菜单
menu

椅子
chair

披萨饼
pizza

汤
soup

桌布
tablecloth

餐具
cutlery

前菜

starter

主菜

main course

甜点

dessert

饮料

drinks

食物

food

瓶子

bottle

快餐

fast food

街边小吃

street food

茶壶

teapot

糖盒

sugar bowl

一份饭菜

portion

意式咖啡机

espresso machine

高脚椅

high chair

账单

bill

托盘

tray

刀

knife

餐叉

fork

勺子

spoon

茶匙

teaspoon

餐巾

serviette

玻璃杯

glass

碟子

plate

汤盘

soup plate

碟子

saucer

酱

sauce

盐瓶

salt pot

胡椒磨

pepper mill

醋

vinegar

食用油

oil

调味料

spices

番茄酱

ketchup

芥末

mustard

蛋黄酱

mayonnaise

超市

supermarket

特价
special offer

顾客
customer

乳制品
dairy

水果
fruit

购物车
trolley

肉铺
butcher's

面包房
baker's

称重
weigh

蔬菜
vegetables

肉
meat

冷冻食品
frozen food

冷盘

cold meat

罐头食品

tinned food

洗衣粉

washing powder

甜食

sweets

日用品

household products

清洁用品

cleaning products

销售员

salesperson

收银机

till

收银员

cashier

购物清单

shopping list

开放时间

opening hours

钱包

wallet

信用卡

credit card

袋子

bag

塑料袋

plastic bag

超市 - supermarket

水

water

果汁

juice

牛奶

milk

可乐

coke

红酒

wine

啤酒

beer

酒

alcohol

可可

cocoa

茶

tea

咖啡

coffee

意式浓缩咖啡

espresso

卡布奇诺

cappuccino

香蕉

banana

苹果

apple

橙子

orange

西瓜

melon

柠檬

lemon

胡萝卜

carrot

大蒜

garlic

竹子

bamboo

洋葱

onion

蘑菇

mushroom

坚果

nuts

面条

noodles

意大利面条

spaghetti

米饭

rice

沙拉

salad

薯条

chips

炸土豆

fried potatoes

披萨饼

pizza

汉堡包

hamburger

三明治

sandwich

炸猪排

cutlet

火腿

ham

萨拉米

salami

香肠

sausage

鸡肉

chicken

烤肉

roast

鱼

fish

燕麦片

porridge oats

穆兹利

muesli

玉米片

cornflakes

面粉

flour

羊角面包

croissant

面包卷

bread roll

面包

bread

烤面包

toast

饼干

biscuits

黄油

butter

凝乳

curd

蛋糕

cake

蛋

egg

煎蛋

fried egg

奶酪

cheese

食物 - food

冰激凌

ice cream

糖

sugar

蜂蜜

honey

果酱

jam

巧克力酱

chocolate spread

咖喱饭

curry

农舍
farmhouse

粮仓
barn

稻草捆
straw bale

田野
field

马
horse

拖车
trailer

马驹
foal

拖拉机
tractor

驴
donkey

羊
sheep

羔羊
lamb

山羊
....
goat

奶牛
....
cow

牛犊
....
calf

猪
....
pig

小猪
....
piglet

公牛
....
bull

鹅

goose

鸭

duck

小鸡

chick

母鸡

hen

公鸡

cock

鼠

rat

猫

cat

老鼠

mouse

牛

ox

狗

dog

狗屋

doghouse

花园浇水软管

garden hose

洒水壶

watering can

长柄大镰刀

scythe

犁

plough

镰刀

sickle

锄头

hoe

长柄草耙

pitchfork

斧头

axe

独轮手推车

wheelbarrow

饲料槽

trough

牛奶罐

milk can

麻布袋

sack

栅栏

fence

马厩

stable

温室

greenhouse

土壤

soil

种子

seed

肥料

fertilizer

联合收割机

combine harvester

收割

harvest

收割

harvest

山药

yams

小麦

wheat

大豆

soy

土豆

potato

玉米

corn

油菜籽

rapeseed

果树

fruit tree

树薯

cassava

谷物

cereals

烟囱
chimney

屋顶
roof

落水管
drainpipe

窗户
window

车库
garage

门铃
doorbell

门
door

垃圾桶
rubbish bin

信箱
letterbox

花园
garden

客厅
living room

浴室
bathroom

厨房
kitchen

卧室
bedroom

儿童房
child's room

餐厅
dining room

地板
floor

墙壁
wall

吊顶
ceiling

地窖
cellar

桑拿
sauna

阳台
balcony

露台
terrace

游泳池
pool

割草机
lawn mower

被单
sheet

床罩
bedspread

床
bed

扫帚
broom

水桶
bucket

开关
switch

壁纸
wallpaper

照片
picture

台灯
lamp

搁架
shelf

橱柜
cupboard

壁炉
fireplace

电视机
television

花
flower

垫子
cushion

花瓶
vase

沙发
sofa

遥控器
remote control

地毯

carpet

窗帘

curtain

餐桌

table

椅子

chair

摇椅

rocking chair

扶手椅

armchair

书

book

毯子

blanket

装饰品

decoration

木柴

firewood

电影

film

高保真音响

hi-fi equipment

钥匙

key

报纸

newspaper

油画

painting

海报

poster

收音机

radio

笔记本

notepad

吸尘器

hoover

仙人掌

cactus

蜡烛

candle

微波炉
microwave oven

冰箱
fridge

厨房秤
kitchen scales

洗洁精
detergent

烤面包机
toaster

烤箱
oven

冰柜
freezer

垃圾桶
rubbish bin

洗碗机
dishwasher

炊具

cooker

锅

pot

铸铁锅

cast-iron pot

炒锅

wok / kadai

平底锅

pan

水壶

kettle

蒸锅

steamer

烤盘

baking tray

陶瓷锅

crockery

马克杯

mug

碗

bowl

筷子

chopsticks

长柄勺

ladle

铲子

spatula

搅拌器

whisk

滤网

strainer

筛子

sieve

磨碎机

grater

研钵

mortar

烧烤

barbecue

明火

open fire

菜板

chopping board

擀面杖

rolling pin

开瓶器

corkscrew

罐子

can

开罐器

can opener

隔热手套

pot holder

水槽

sink

刷子

brush

海绵

sponge

搅拌机

blender

冷藏箱

deep freezer

奶瓶

baby bottle

水龙头

tap

浴室
bathroom

供暖设备
heating

淋浴
shower

毛巾
towel

泡沫浴
bubble bath

浴帘
shower curtain

浴缸
bathtub

洗衣机
washing machine

玻璃杯
glass

瓷砖
tiles

水龙头
tap

便壶
potty

水槽
sink

厕所
toilet

蹲便器
squat toilet

坐浴器
bidet

小便池
urinal

厕纸
toilet paper

马桶刷
toilet brush

牙刷
toothbrush

牙膏
toothpaste

牙线
dental floss

洗
wash

手持式喷淋头
handheld shower

冲洗器
douche

洗脸盆
basin

擦背刷
back brush

肥皂
soap

沐浴露
shower gel

洗发水
shampoo

法兰绒
flannel

排水
drain

乳霜
cream

除臭剂
deodorant

镜子

mirror

手镜

hand mirror

剃须刀

razor

剃须泡沫

shaving foam

须后水

aftershave

梳子

comb

刷子

brush

吹风机

hair dryer

喷发定型剂

hairspray

化妆品

makeup

唇膏

lipstick

指甲油

nail varnish

化妆棉

cotton wool

指甲剪

nail scissors

香水

perfume

洗漱包

washbag

凳子

stool

计重秤

weighing scale

浴袍

bathrobe

橡胶手套

rubber gloves

卫生棉条

tampon

卫生巾

sanitary towel

化学厕所

chemical toilet

闹钟
alarm clock

毛绒玩具
cuddly toy

玩具车
toy car

拨浪鼓
rattle

玩具屋
doll's house

礼物
present

气球
balloon

床
bed

（洋娃娃用）婴儿车
pram

扑克牌
deck of cards

拼图
jigsaw

漫画
comic

乐高积木

lego bricks

积木玩具

building blocks

玩具人

action figure

婴儿服

babygrow

飞盘

frisbee

床铃玩具

mobile

棋盘游戏

board game

骰子

dice

火车模型

model train set

安抚奶嘴

dummy

聚会

party

绘本

picture book

球

ball

洋娃娃

doll

玩

play

沙坑

sandpit

秋千

swing

玩具

toys

游戏机

video game console

三轮车

tricycle

泰迪熊

teddy bear

衣柜

wardrobe

衣服
clothing

袜子

socks

长袜

stockings

紧身裤

tights

围巾
scarf

雨伞
umbrella

T恤
t-shirt

皮带
belt

靴子
boots

拖鞋
slippers

运动鞋
trainers

凉鞋
sandals

鞋
shoes

雨靴
rubber boots

内裤
underpants

胸罩
bra

背心
vest

衣服 - clothing

身体
body

裤子
trousers

牛仔裤
jeans

短裙
skirt

女式衬衫
blouse

衬衫
shirt

套头衫
pullover

卫衣
hoodie

西装夹克
blazer

夹克
jacket

外套
coat

雨衣
raincoat

套装
costume

连衣裙
dress

婚纱
wedding dress

西装
suit

睡袍
nightgown

睡衣
pyjamas

莎丽
sari

头巾
headscarf

包头巾
turban

波卡
burqa

卡夫坦
kaftan

(阿拉伯式)长袍长袍
abaya

泳衣
swimsuit

男式泳裤
trunks

短裤
shorts

运动服
tracksuit

围裙
apron

手套
gloves

衣服 - clothing

纽扣

button

眼镜

glasses

手链

bracelet

项链

necklace

戒指

ring

耳环

earring

便帽

cap

衣架

coat hanger

帽子

hat

领带

tie

拉链

zip

头盔

helmet

背带

braces

校服

school uniform

制服

uniform

围兜
bib

安抚奶嘴
dummy

尿不湿
nappy

服务器
server

文件柜
filing cabinet

打印机
printer

显示屏
monitor

纸
paper

鼠标
mouse

办公桌
desk

文件夹
folder

键盘
keyboard

椅子
chair

废纸筐
waste-paper basket

电脑
computer

咖啡杯
coffee mug

计算器
calculator

因特网
internet

笔记本电脑
laptop

信件
letter

消息
message

手机
mobile

网络
network

复印机
photocopier

软件
software

电话
telephone

插座
plug socket

传真机
fax machine

表格
form

文件
document

买

buy

付钱

pay

交易

trade

现金

money

美元

dollar

欧元

euro

日元

yen

卢布

rouble

瑞士法郎

Swiss franc

人民币

renminbi yuan

卢比

rupee

提款处

cashpoint

外币兑换处

bureau de change

金

gold

银

silver

石油

oil

能源

energy

价格

price

合同

contract

税金

tax

股票

stock

工作

work

职员

employee

老板

employer

工厂

factory

商店

shop

警官
police officer

消防员
fireman

厨师
cook

医生
doctor

飞行员
pilot

园丁

gardener

木匠

carpenter

裁缝

seamstress

法官

judge

化学家

chemist

演员

actor

公交车司机

bus driver

出租车司机

taxi driver

渔夫

fisherman

清洁女工

cleaning lady

屋顶工

roofer

服务员

waiter

猎人

hunter

画家

painter

面包师

baker

电工

electrician

建筑工人

builder

工程师

engineer

屠夫

butcher

水管工

plumber

邮递员

postman

士兵

soldier

建筑师

architect

收银员

cashier

花农

florist

理发师

hairdresser

售票员

conductor

机械师

mechanic

船长

captain

牙医

dentist

科学家

scientist

拉比

rabbi

伊玛目

imam

和尚

monk

牧师

clergyman

铁锤
hammer

钳子
pliers

螺丝刀
screwdriver

扳手
spanner

手电筒
torch

挖掘机

digger

工具箱

toolbox

梯子

ladder

锯子

saw

钉子

nails

钻机

drill

修
repair

铲子
shovel

靠！
Damn!

簸箕
dustpan

油漆桶
paint pot

螺丝
screws

乐器
musical instruments

打击乐器
drum kit ◣

扬声器
loudspeaker

低音提琴
double bass

小号
trumpet

吉他
guitar ◣

钢琴

piano

小提琴

violin

贝斯

bass

定音鼓

timpani

鼓

drums

电子琴

keyboard

萨克斯管

saxophone

长笛

flute

麦克风

microphone

入口
entrance

老虎
tiger

笼子
cage

斑马
zebra

动物饲料
animal feed

熊猫
panda

动物

animals

大象

elephant

袋鼠

kangaroo

犀牛

rhino

大猩猩

gorilla

熊

bear

骆驼

camel

鸵鸟

ostrich

狮子

lion

猴子

monkey

火烈鸟

flamingo

鹦鹉

parrot

北极熊

polar bear

企鹅

penguin

鲨鱼

shark

孔雀

peacock

蛇

snake

鳄鱼

crocodile

动物园管理员

zookeeper

海豹

seal

美洲豹

jaguar

矮种马

pony

豹

leopard

河马

hippo

长颈鹿

giraffe

老鹰

eagle

野猪

boar

鱼

fish

龟

turtle

海象

walrus

狐狸

fox

羚羊

gazelle

橄榄球
American football

骑自行车
cycling

网球
tennis

篮球
basketball

游泳
swimming

拳击
boxing

冰球
ice hockey

英式足球
football

羽毛球
badminton

田径
athletics

手球
handball

滑雪
skiing

马球
polo

跳
jump

笑
laugh

拥抱
hug

走路
walk

唱
sing

做梦
dream

祈祷
pray

亲吻
kiss

书写
write

画
draw

展示
show

推
push

给
give

拿
take

有

have

做

do

当

be

站

stand

跑

run

拉

pull

扔

throw

摔倒

fall

躺

lie

等待

wait

携带

carry

坐

sit

穿衣

get dressed

睡觉

sleep

醒来

wake up

看
look at

哭
cry

抚摸
stroke

梳头
comb

交谈
talk

明白
understand

问
ask

听
listen

喝
drink

吃
eat

清理
tidy up

爱
love

做饭
cook

开车
drive

飞
fly

活动 - activities

航行

sail

计算

calculate

读

read

学习

learn

工作

work

结婚

marry

缝

sew

刷牙

brush teeth

杀

kill

抽烟

smoke

寄

send

祖母
grandmother

婴童
baby

母亲
mother

祖父
grandfather

父亲
father

女儿
daughter

儿子
son

客人

guest

阿姨

aunt

叔叔

uncle

兄弟

brother

姐妹

sister

前额
forehead

眼睛
eye

肩膀
shoulder

手指
finger

脸
face

下巴
chin

手
hand

乳房
breast

手臂
arm

腿
leg

婴童
baby

男人
man

女人
woman

女孩
girl

男孩
boy

头
head

背部

back

肚子

belly

肚脐

belly button

脚趾

toe

脚后跟

heel

骨头

bone

臀部

hip

膝盖

knee

手肘

elbow

鼻子

nose

屁股

bottom

皮肤

skin

脸颊

cheek

耳朵

ear

嘴唇

lip

身体 - body

嘴

mouth

牙齿

tooth

舌头

tongue

脑

brain

心脏

heart

肌肉

muscle

肺

lung

肝脏

liver

胃

stomach

肾脏

kidneys

性交

sex

避孕套

condom

卵子

ovum

精子

semen

怀孕

pregnancy

月经

menstruation

阴道

vagina

阴茎

penis

眉毛

eyebrow

头发

hair

脖子

neck

医院
hospital

救护车
ambulance

轮椅
wheelchair

骨折
fracture

医生
doctor

急诊室
emergency room

护士
nurse

紧急情况
emergency

昏迷
unconscious

痛
pain

受伤
injury

出血
bleeding

心脏病发作
heart attack

中风
stroke

过敏
allergy

咳嗽
cough

发烧
fever

流感
flu

腹泻
diarrhoea

头痛
headache

癌症
cancer

糖尿病
diabetes

外科医生
surgeon

手术刀
scalpel

手术
operation

CT

CT

X光

x-ray

超声波

ultrasound

口罩

face mask

疾病

disease

候诊室

waiting room

拐杖

crutch

石膏

plaster

绷带

bandage

注射

injection

听诊器

stethoscope

担架

stretcher

体温计

clinical thermometer

出生

birth

超重

overweight

助听器

hearing aid

消毒液

disinfectant

感染

infection

病毒

virus

艾滋病

HIV / AIDS

药物

medicine

接种疫苗

vaccination

药片

tablets

药丸

pill

急救电话

emergency call

血压计

blood pressure monitor

生病/健康

ill / healthy

救命！
Help!

警报
alarm

突击
assault

攻击
attack

危险
danger

紧急出口
emergency exit

着火啦！
Fire!

灭火器
fire extinguisher

意外
accident

急救箱
first-aid kit

呼救信号
SOS

警察
police

欧洲

Europe

北美洲

North America

南美洲

South America

非洲

Africa

亚洲

Asia

澳洲

Australia

大西洋

Atlantic

太平洋

Pacific

印度洋

Indian Ocean

南冰洋

Antarctic Ocean

北冰洋

Arctic Ocean

北极

North Pole

南极
South Pole

南极洲
Antarctica

地球
Earth

陆地
land

海
sea

岛
island

国家
nation

国家
state

钟面

clock face

时针

hour hand

分针

minute hand

秒针

second hand

现在几点？

What time is it?

天

day

时间

time

现在

now

电子表

digital watch

分

minute

时

hour

周

week

周一 Monday
周三 Wednesday
周五 Friday
周二 Tuesday
周四 Thursday
周六 Saturday
周日 Sunday

昨天

yesterday

今天

today

明天

tomorrow

早晨

morning

中午

noon

晚上

evening

工作日

business days

周末

weekend

雨
rain

彩虹
rainbow

风
wind

雪
snow

春
spring

夏
summer

秋
autumn

冬
winter

天气预报
weather forecast

温度计
thermometer

阳光
sunshine

云
cloud

雾
fog

潮湿
humidity

闪电

lightning

打雷

thunder

风暴

storm

冰雹

hail

季风

monsoon

洪水

flood

冰

ice

一月

January

二月

February

三月

March

四月

April

五月

May

六月

June

七月

July

八月

August

九月

September

十月

October

十一月

November

十二月

December

圆形

circle

正方形

square

长方形

rectangle

三角形

triangle

球体

sphere

立方体

cube

形状 - shapes

白

white

黄

yellow

橙

orange

粉

pink

红

red

紫

purple

蓝

blue

绿

green

棕

brown

灰

grey

黑

black

很多/少许

a lot / a little

生气/平静

angry / calm

美/丑

beautiful / ugly

首/尾

beginning / end

大/小

big / small

明/暗

bright / dark

兄弟/姐妹

brother / sister

干净/肮脏

clean / dirty

完整/缺失

complete / incomplete

白天/晚上

day / night

死/生

dead / alive

宽/窄

wide / narrow

可食用/非食用

edible / inedible

邪恶/善良

evil / kind

兴奋/无聊

excited / bored

胖/瘦

fat / thin

第一/最后

first / last

朋友/敌人

friend / enemy

满/空

full / empty

硬/软

hard / soft

重/轻

heavy / light

饿/渴

hunger / thirst

生病/健康

ill / healthy

非法/合法

illegal / legal

聪明/愚笨

intelligent / stupid

左/右

left / right

近/远

near / far

新/旧

new / used

没有/有些

nothing / something

老/幼

old / young

开/关

on / off

打开/合上

open / closed

安静/吵闹

quiet / loud

富/穷

rich / poor

对/错

right / wrong

粗糙/光滑

rough / smooth

伤心/高兴

sad / happy

短/长

short / long

慢/快

slow / fast

湿/干

wet / dry

温暖/凉爽

warm / cool

战争/和平

war / peace

0

零
zero

1

一
one

2

二
two

3

三
three

4

四
four

5

五
five

6

六
six

7

七
seven

8

八
eight

9

九
nine

10

十
ten

11

十一
eleven

12

十二
....
twelve

13

十三
....
thirteen

14

十四
....
fourteen

15

十五
....
fifteen

16

十六
....
sixteen

17

十七
....
seventeen

18

十八
....
eighteen

19

十九
....
nineteen

20

二十
....
twenty

100

百
....
hundred

1.000

千
....
thousand

1.000.000

百万
....
million

英语
English

美式英语
American English

普通话
Chinese Mandarin

印地语
Hindi

西班牙语
Spanish

法语
French

阿拉伯语
Arabic

俄语
Russian

葡萄牙语
Portuguese

孟加拉语
Bengali

德语
German

日语
Japanese

我

I

你

you

他/她/它

he / she / it

我们

we

你们

you

他们

they

谁？

who?

什么？

what?

怎样？

how?

哪里？

where?

什么时候？

when?

名字

name

后面

behind

里面

in

前面

in front of

上方

over

上面

on

下面

under

旁边

beside

中间

between

地点

place